T0088561

SEQUENTIAL

Disney PIANO SONGS

Disney characters and Artwork © 2019 Disney

ISBN 978-1-5400-5439-5

Visit Hal Leonard Online at
www.halleonard.com

Contact us:
Hal Leonard
7777 West Bluemound Road
Milwaukee, WI 53213
Email: info@halleonard.com

In Europe, contact:
Hal Leonard Europe Limited
42 Wigmore Street
Marylebone, London, W1U 2RN
Email: info@halleonardeurope.com

In Australia, contact:
Hal Leonard Australia Pty. Ltd.
4 Lentara Court
Cheltenham, Victoria, 3192 Australia
Email: info@halleonard.com.au

The 24 songs in this book are presented in a basic order of difficulty, beginning with the easiest arrangements (hands alone, very simple rhythms) and progressing to more difficult arrangements including hands together, syncopated rhythms and moving around the keyboard.

SUPERCALIFRAGILISTICEXPIALIDOCIOUS
from MARY POPPINS

Words and Music by RICHARD M. SHERMAN
and ROBERT B. SHERMAN

Brightly

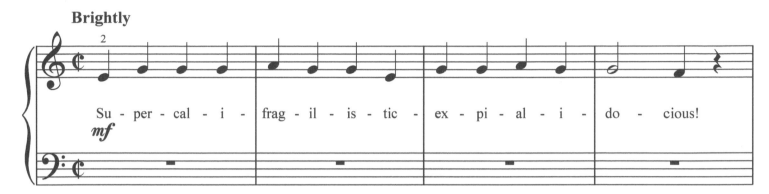

Su - per - cal - i - frag - il - is - tic - ex - pi - al - i - do - cious!

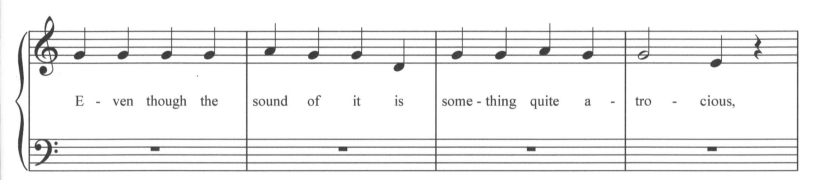

E - ven though the sound of it is some - thing quite a - tro - cious,

if you say it loud e - nough, you'll al - ways sound pre - co - cious.

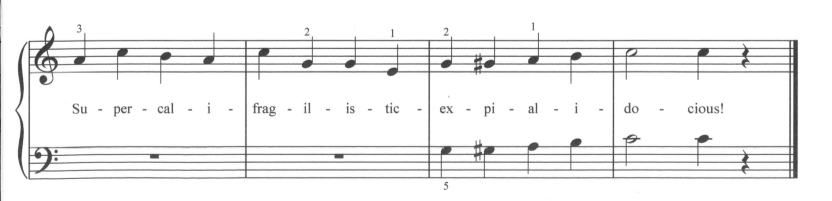

Su - per - cal - i - frag - il - is - tic - ex - pi - al - i - do - cious!

IT'S A SMALL WORLD

from Disney Parks' "it's a small world" attraction

Words and Music by RICHARD M. SHERMAN
and ROBERT B. SHERMAN

Brisk March tempo

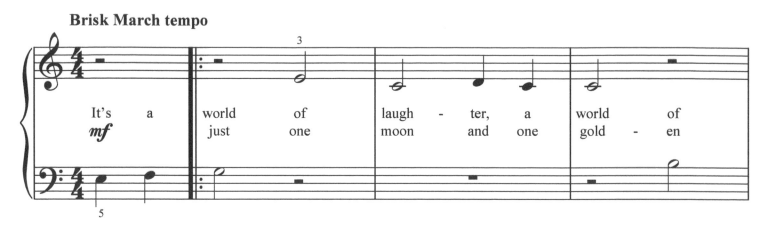

It's a world just of one laugh - ter, a moon and a one world gold - en

mf

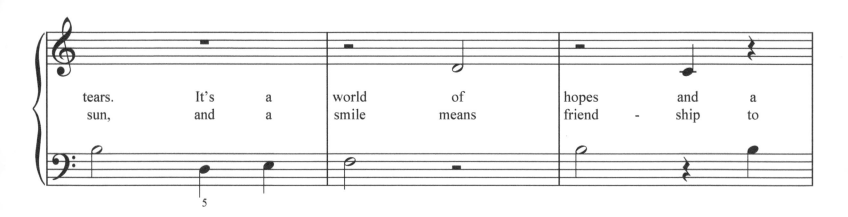

tears. It's a world of hopes and a
sun, and a smile means friend - ship to

world ev - 'ry -

world of fears. There's so much that we
ev - 'ry - one. Though the moun - tians di -

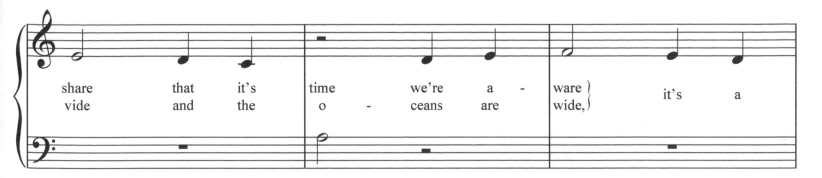

share   that   it's   time   we're   a -   ware   it's   a
vide   and   the   o -   ceans   are   wide,

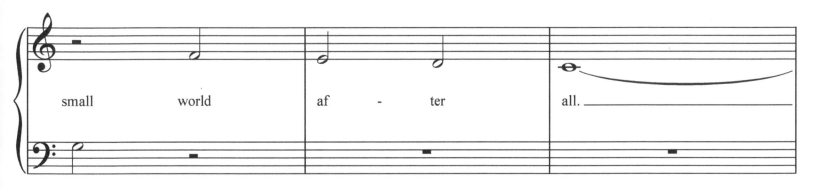

small   world   af   -   ter   all. _____

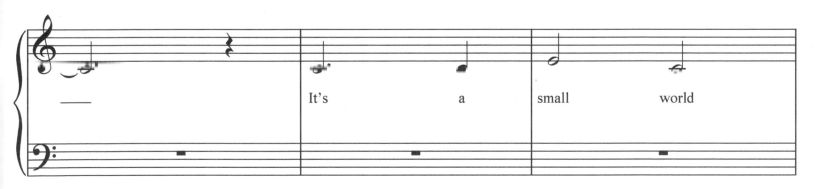

_____   It's   a   small   world

af   -   ter   all.   It's   a

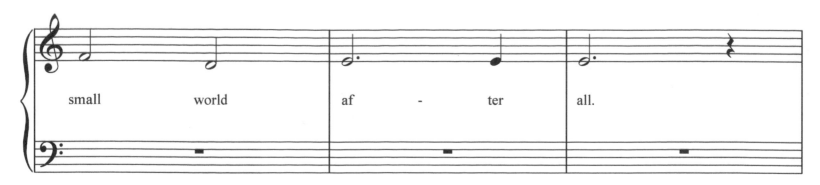

small   world   af - ter   all.

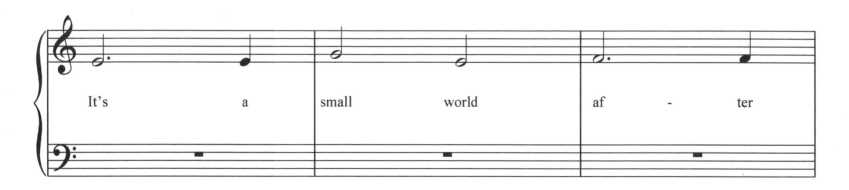

It's   a   small   world   af - ter

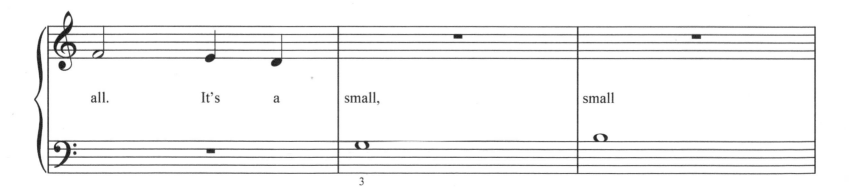

all.   It's   a   small,   small

3

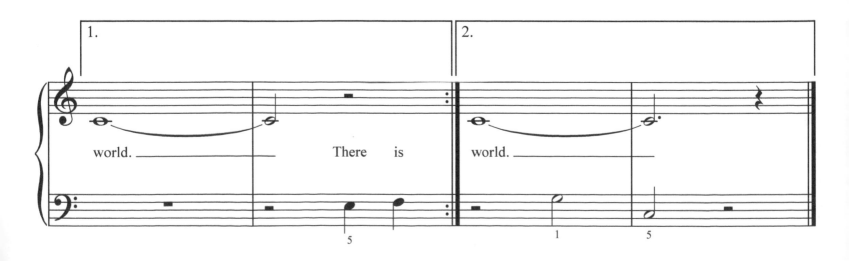

1.

world. _____   There   is

2.

world. _____

5   1   5

BE OUR GUEST

from BEAUTY AND THE BEAST

Music by ALAN MENKEN
Lyrics by HOWARD ASHMAN

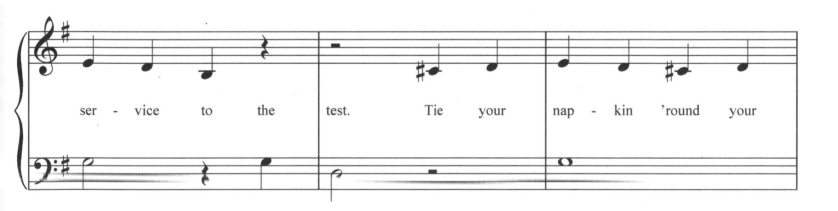

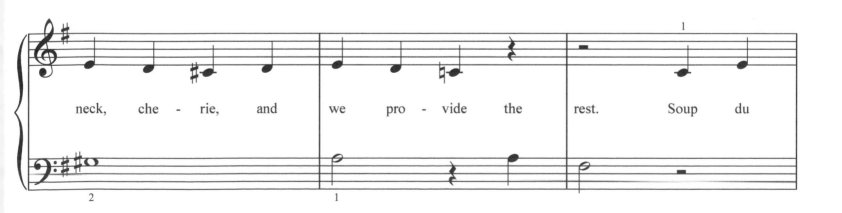

jour! Hot hors d'oeuvres! Why, we on - ly live to

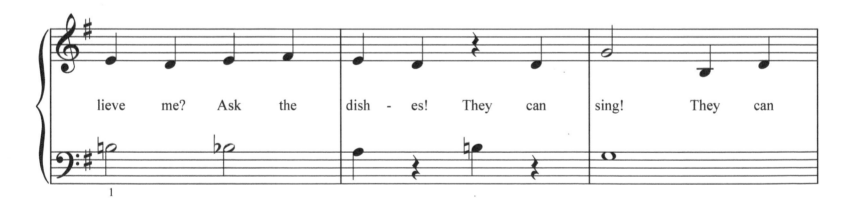

serve. Try the grey stuff, it's de - li - cious! Don't be -

lieve me? Ask the dish - es! They can sing! They can

dance! Af - ter all, Miss, this is France! And a

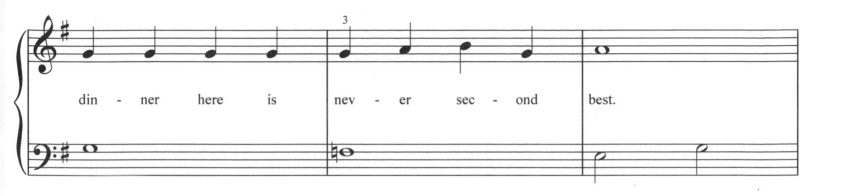

din - ner here is nev - er sec - ond best.

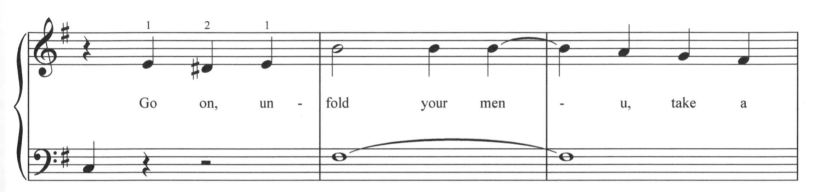

Go on, un - fold your men - u, take a

glance, and then you'll be our guest, oui, our

guest! Be our guest! _____

A DREAM IS A WISH
YOUR HEART MAKES

from CINDERELLA

Music by MACK DAVID and AL HOFFMAN
Lyrics by JERRY LIVINGSTON

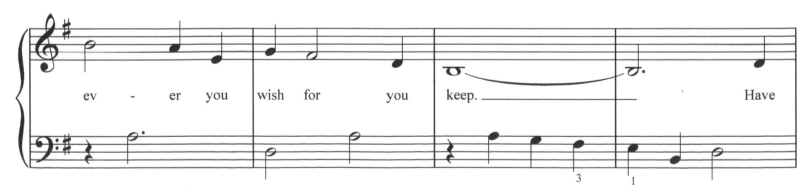

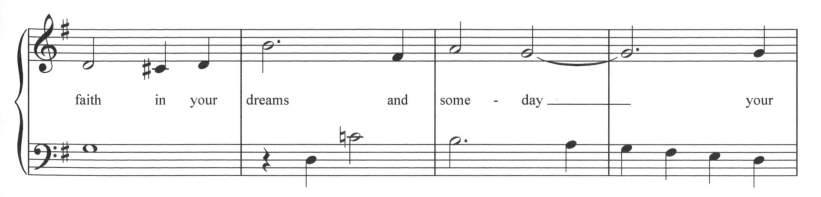

faith in your dreams and some - day _____ your

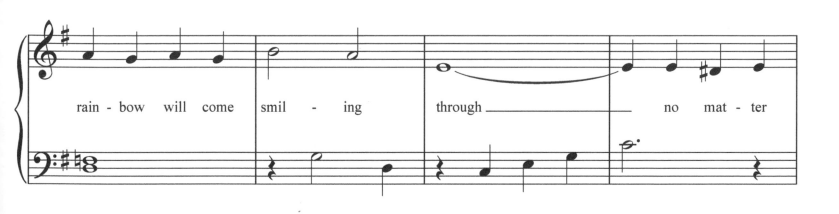

rain - bow will come smil - ing through _____ no mat - ter

how your heart is griev - ing, if you keep on be - liev - ing, the

dream that you wish will come true. _____

REINDEER(S) ARE BETTER THAN PEOPLE

from FROZEN

Music and Lyrics by KRISTEN ANDERSON-LOPEZ
and ROBERT LOPEZ

Freely

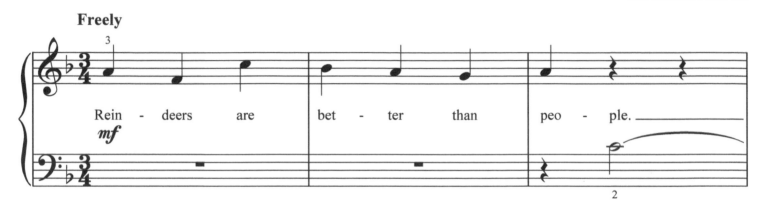

Rein - deers are bet - ter than peo - ple. _____

_____ Sven, don't you think that's

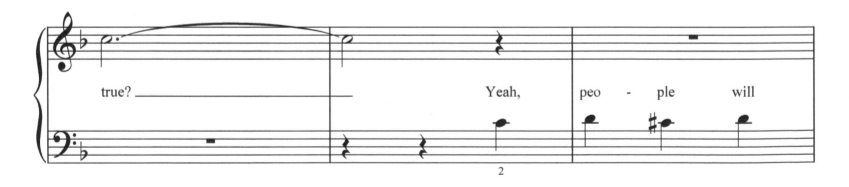

true? _____ Yeah, peo - ple will

beat you and curse you and cheat you. Ev - 'ry

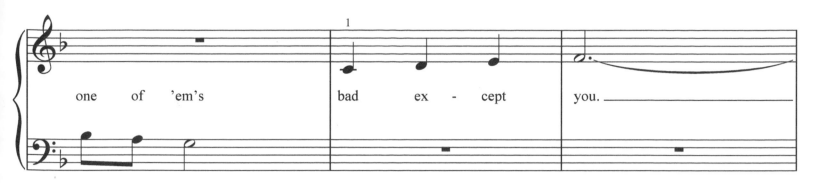

one of 'em's   bad   ex -   cept   you. _____

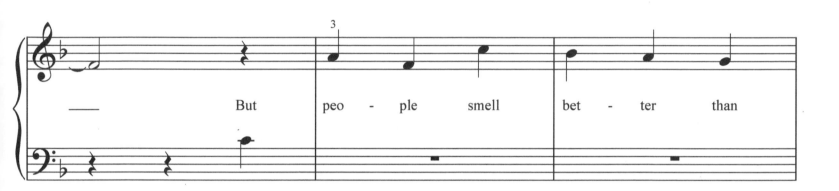

_____   But   peo -   ple   smell   bet -   ter   than

rein -   deers. _____   Sven,   don't   you

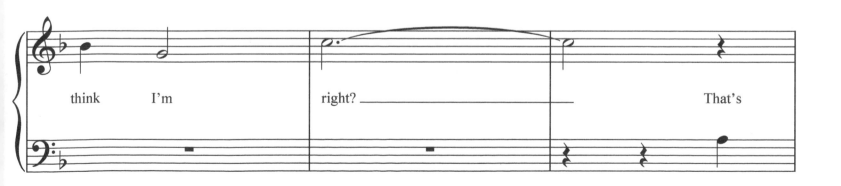

think   I'm   right? _____   That's

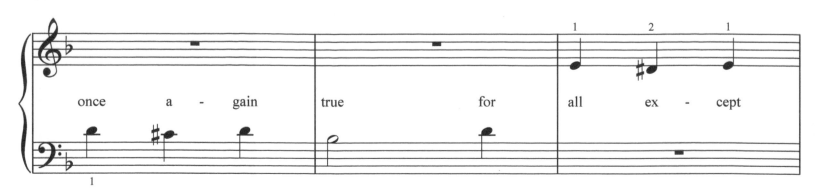

once a - gain true for all ex - cept

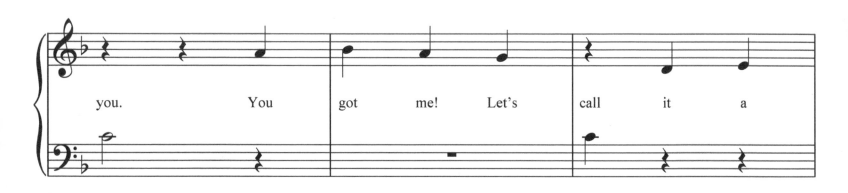

you. You got me! Let's call it a

night. Good night! Don't let the

frost - bite bite.

I SEE THE LIGHT
from TANGLED

Music by ALAN MENKEN
Lyrics by GLENN SLATER

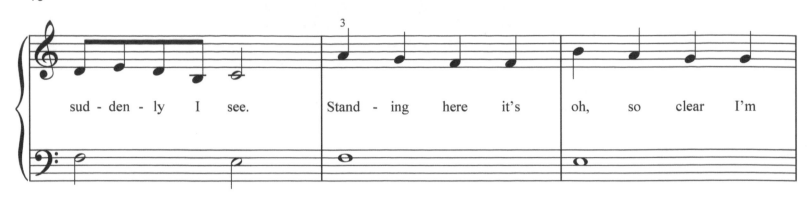

sud - den - ly I see. Stand - ing here it's oh, so clear I'm

where I'm meant to be. And at last I see the

light, and it's like the fog has lift - ed. And at

last I see the light, and it's like the sky is

new.   And it's   warm   and   real   and   bright,   and the

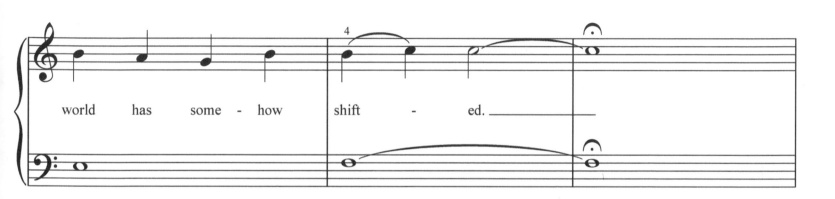

world   has   some - how   shift -   ed. _____

All   at   once,   ev - 'ry - thing   is   dif - f'rent,   now   that   I   see

you.   Now   that   I   see   you.

REMEMBER ME
(Ernesto de la Cruz)
from COCO

Music and Lyrics by KRISTEN ANDERSON-LOPEZ
and ROBERT LOPEZ

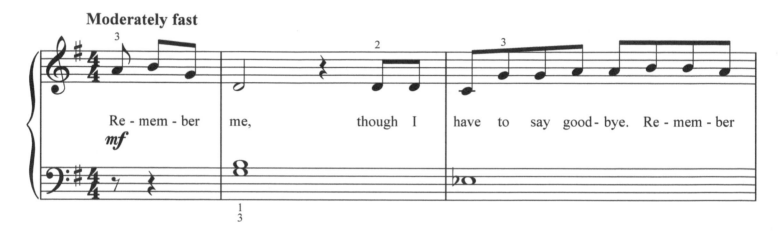

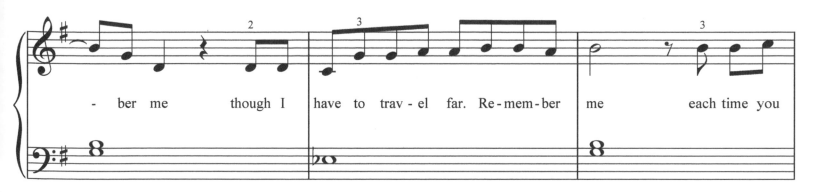

- ber me   though I have to trav - el far. Re - mem - ber   me   each time you

hear a   sad gui - tar.   Know that I'm with you the on - ly   way that I can be.

Un - til you're in my arms a - gain,   re - mem - ber   me.

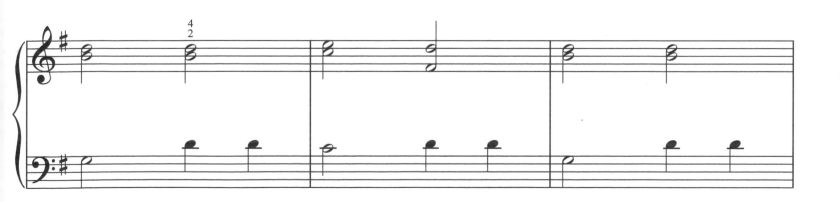

Re - mem - ber me, though I

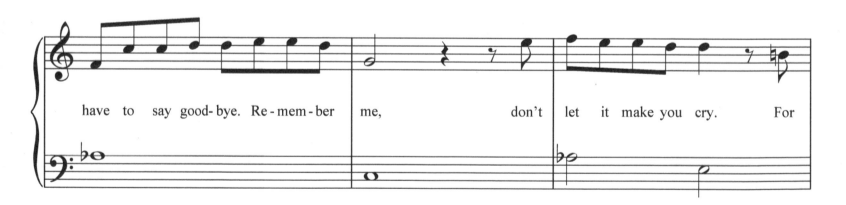

have to say good-bye. Re-mem-ber me, don't let it make you cry. For

e - ven if I'm far a - way, I hold you in my heart. I sing a se - cret song to you each

night we are a-part. Re-mem - ber me though I have to trav-el far. Re-mem-ber

me each time you hear a sad gui-tar. Know that I'm with you the on-ly

Slowly, deliberately

way that I can be. *rall.* Un-til you're in my arms a-gain, re-

mem - ber me. _____

ZIP-A-DEE-DOO-DAH
from SONG OF THE SOUTH

Words by RAY GILBERT
Music by ALLIE WRUBEL

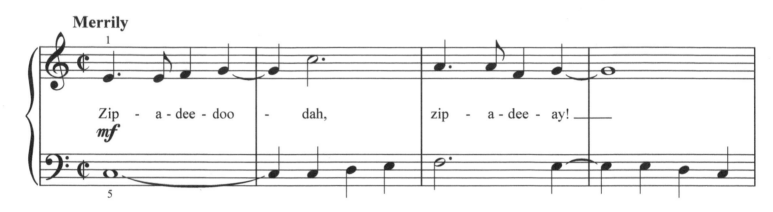

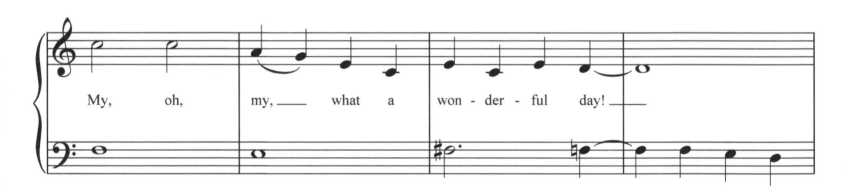

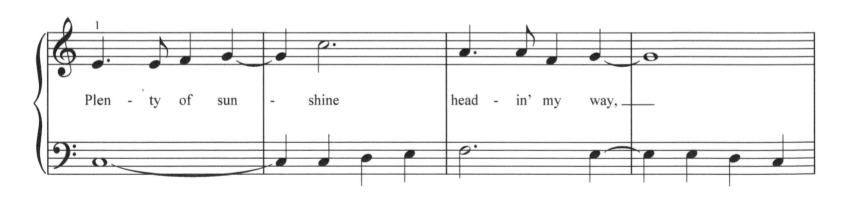

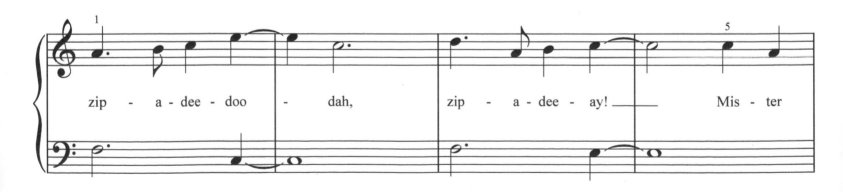

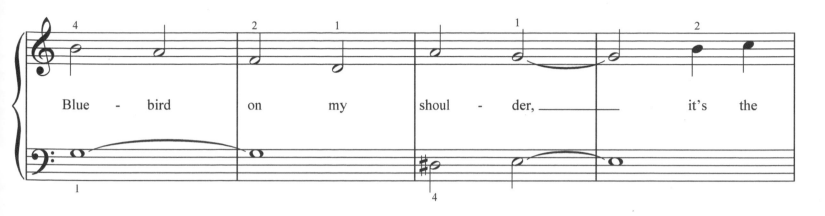

Blue - bird on my shoul - der, _____ it's the

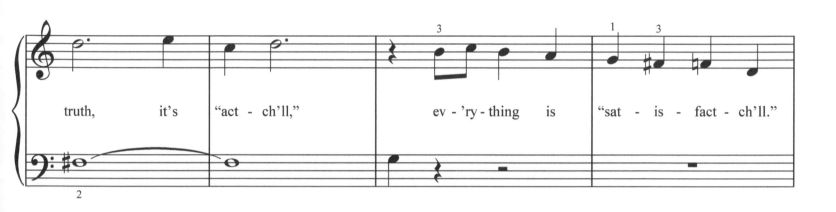

truth, it's "act - ch'll," ev - 'ry - thing is "sat - is - fact - ch'll."

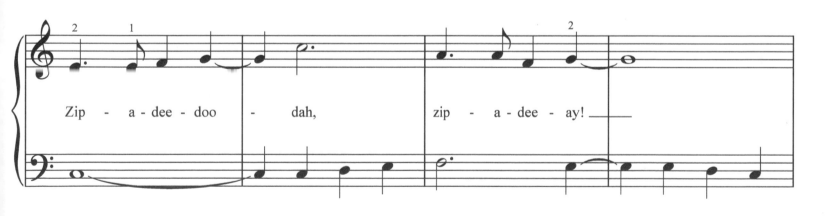

Zip - a - dee - doo - dah, zip - a - dee - ay! _____

Won - der - ful feel - ing, won - der - ful day. _____

EVERMORE
from BEAUTY AND THE BEAST

Music by ALAN MENKEN
Lyrics by TIM RICE

Moderately slow, with freedom

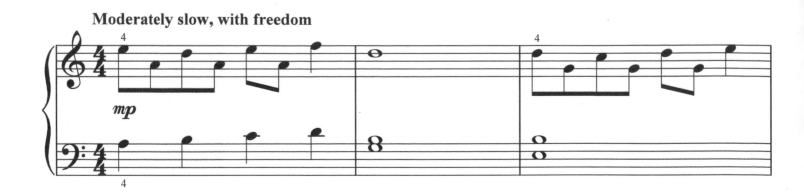

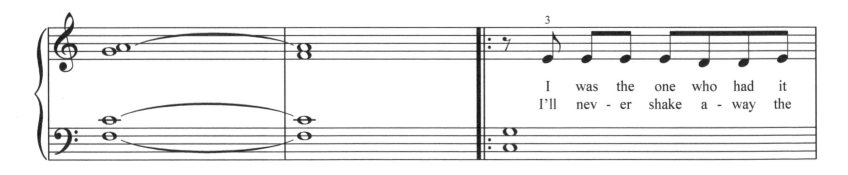

I was the one who had it
I'll nev - er shake a - way the

all;
pain.

I was the mas - ter of my
I close my eyes, but she's still

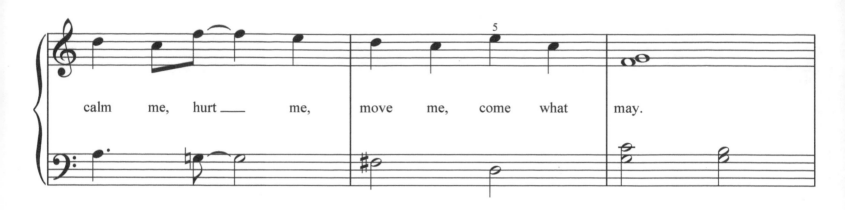

calm me, hurt _____ me, move me, come what may.

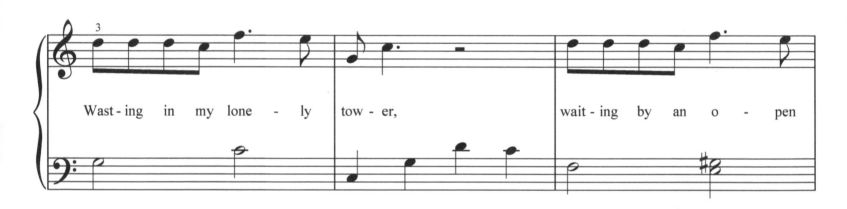

Wast-ing in my lone - ly tow - er, wait - ing by an o - pen

door, I'll fool my - self she'll walk right in,

and be with me for - ev - er - more.

I rage a-gainst the trials of love. I curse the fad-ing of the

light. Though she's al-read-y flown so far be-yond my reach,

she's nev-er out of sight. Now I

know she'll nev-er leave me, e-ven as she fades from

28

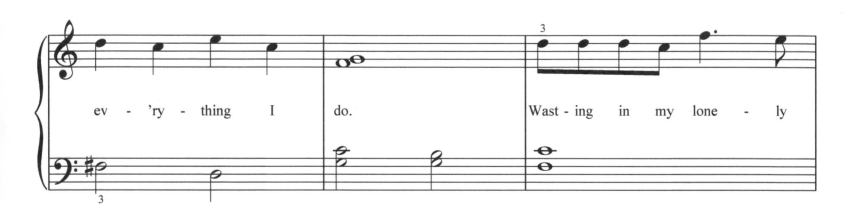

view.　　She will still in - spire me, be a part ___ of

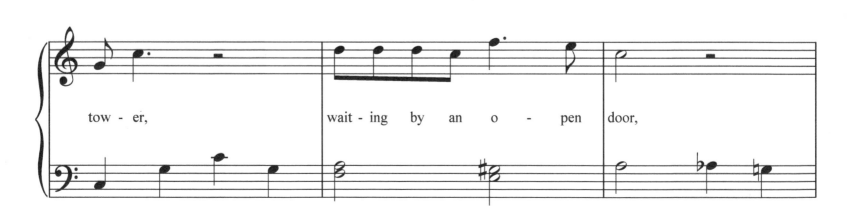

ev - 'ry - thing I do.　　Wast - ing in my lone - ly

tow - er,　waiting by an o - pen door,

I'll fool my - self she'll walk right in,

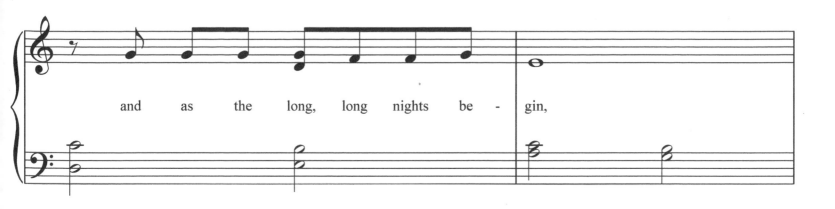

and as the long, long nights be - gin,

I'll think of all that might have been, wait - ing

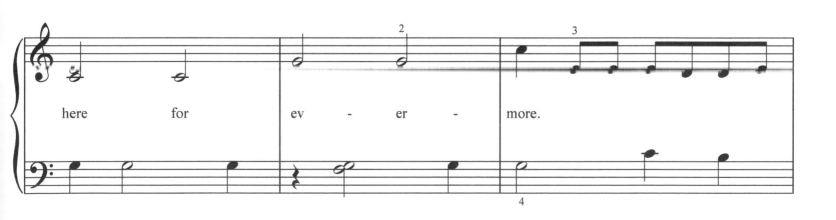

here for ev - er - more.

A SPOONFUL OF SUGAR

from MARY POPPINS

Words and Music by RICHARD M. SHERMAN
and ROBERT B. SHERMAN

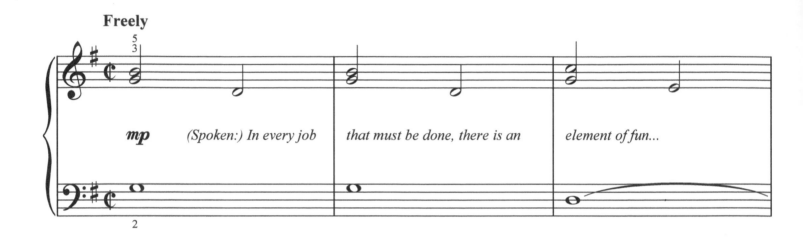

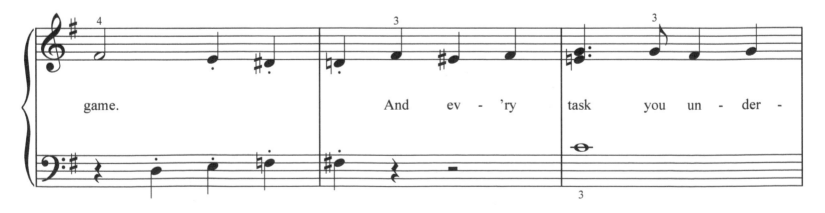

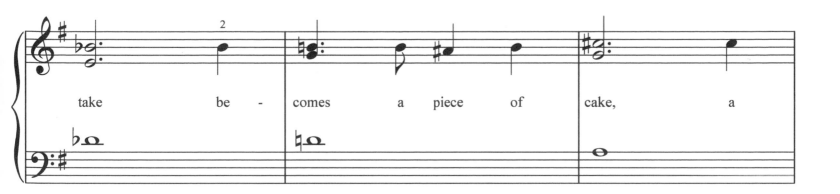

take be - comes a piece of cake, a

lark, a spree! It's ver - y clear to

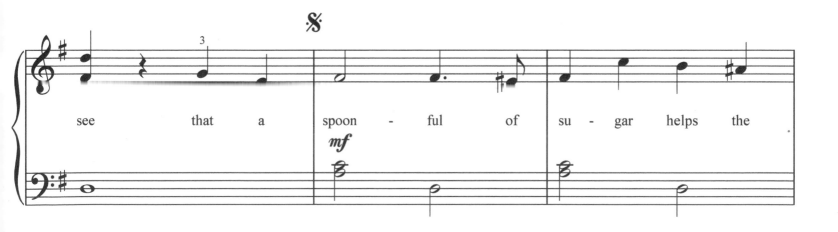

see that a spoon - ful of su - gar helps the

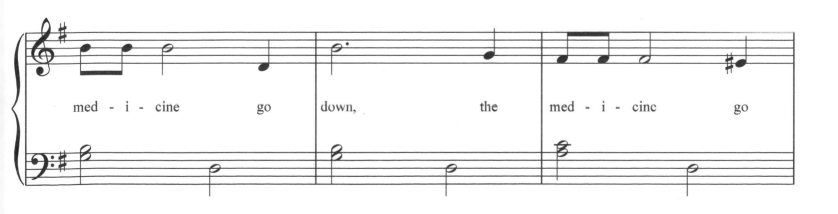

med - i - cine go down, the med - i - cine go

down, _____ med - i - cine go down. Just a

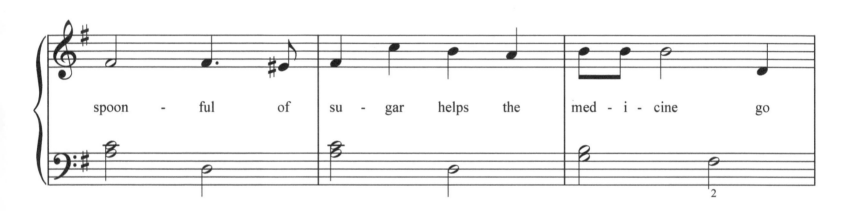

spoon - ful of su - gar helps the med - i - cine go

To Coda ⊕

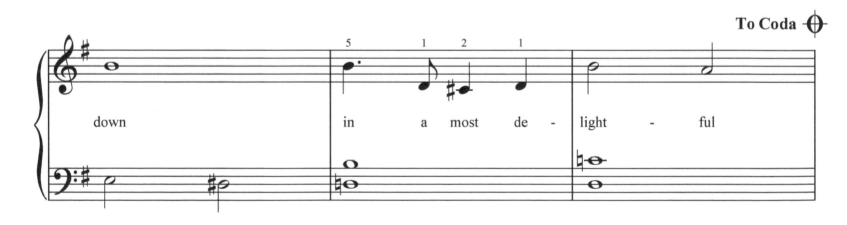

down in a most de - light - ful

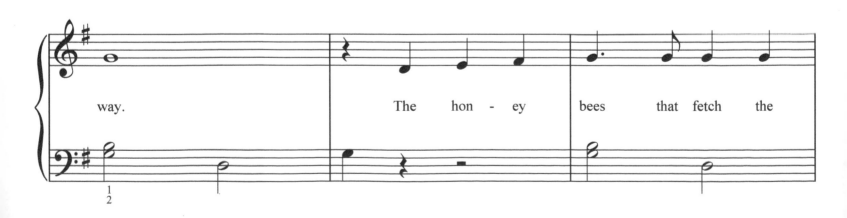

way. The hon - ey bees that fetch the

nec - tar from the flow - ers to the comb nev - er

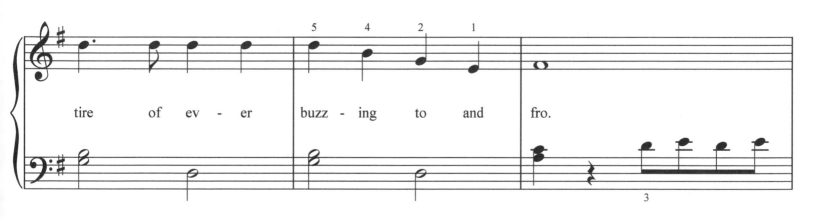

tire of ev - er buzz - ing to and fro.

Be - cause they take a lit - tle nip from ev - 'ry

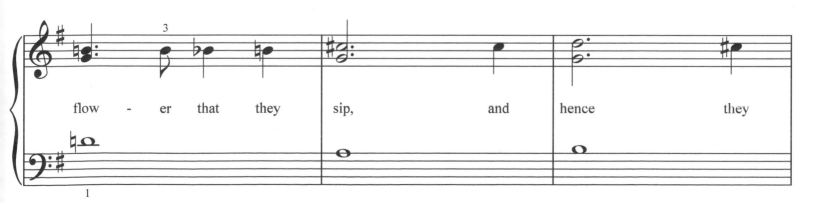

flow - er that they sip, and hence they

D.S. al Coda

find their task is not a grind. For a

CODA

in a most de - light - ful, in a most

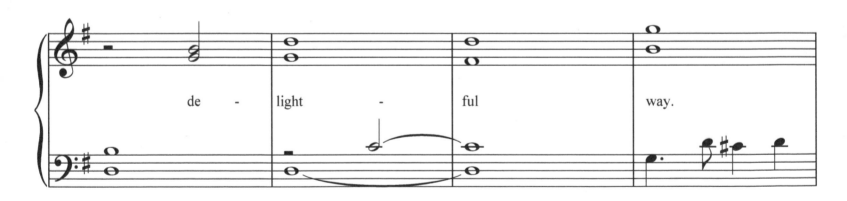

de - light - ful way.

CHIM CHIM CHER-EE

from MARY POPPINS

Words and Music by RICHARD M. SHERMAN
and ROBERT B. SHERMAN

Lightly, with gusto

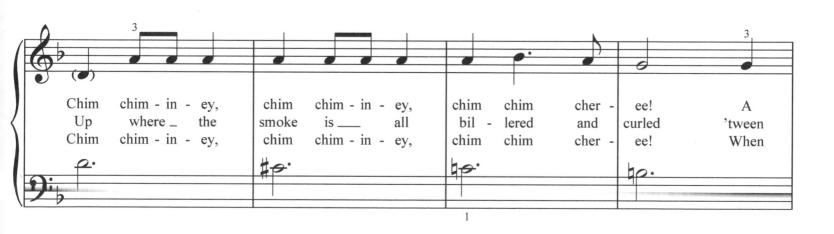

Chim chim-in-ey, chim chim-in-ey, chim chim cher- ee! A
Up where _ the smoke is __ all bil - lered and curled 'tween
Chim chim-in-ey, chim chim-in-ey, chim chim cher - ee! When

sweep is as luck - y as luck - y can be.
pave - ment and stars is the chim - ney sweep world. When there's
you're with a sweep you're in glad com - pa - ny.

Chim chim-in-ey, chim chim-in-ey, chim chim cher- oo! Good
'ard - ly __ no day __ nor 'ard - ly no night, there's
No - where __ is there a more 'ap - pi - er crew than

To Coda ⊕

luck will rub off when I shake 'ands with you, or
things 'alf in shad - ow and 'alf - way in light, on the
them wot sings "chim chim cher - ee, chim cher - oo!"

blow me a kiss and that's luck - y too.
roof - tops of Lon - don; coo, what a sight!

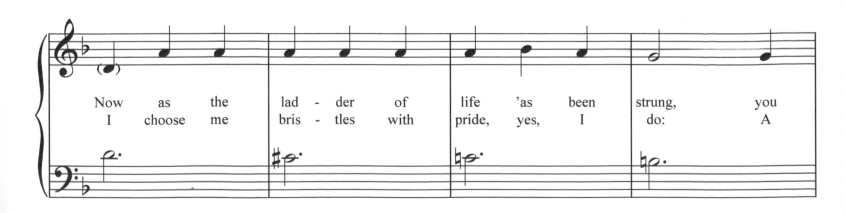

Now as the lad - der of life 'as been strung, you
I choose me bris - tles with pride, yes, I do: A

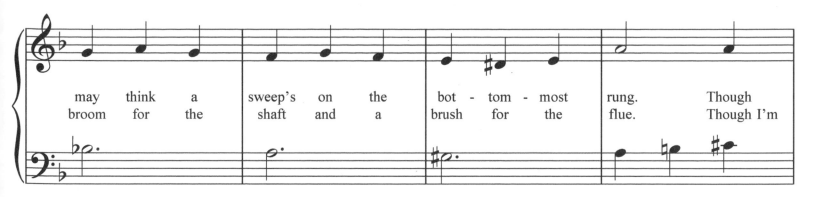

may think a | sweep's on the | bot - tom - most | rung. Though
broom for the | shaft and a | brush for the | flue. Though I'm

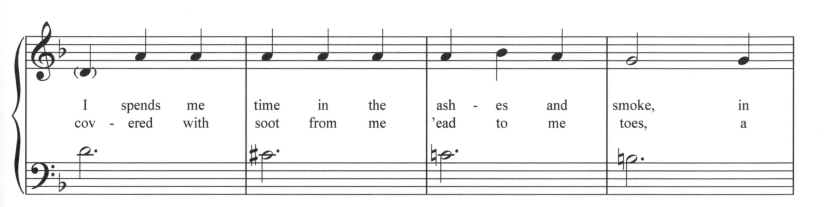

I spends me | time in the | ash - es and | smoke, in
cov - ered with | soot from me | 'ead to me | toes, a

1st time: D.C.
2nd time: D.C. al Coda

this 'ole wide | world there's no | 'ap - pi - er | bloke.
sweep knows 'e's | wel - come wher - | ev - er 'e | goes.

CODA

Chim chim - in - ey | chim chim, cher - ee, | chim cher - oo!

A WHOLE NEW WORLD
(Aladdin's Theme)
from ALADDIN

Music by ALAN MENKEN
Lyrics by TIM RICE

Slowly and sweetly

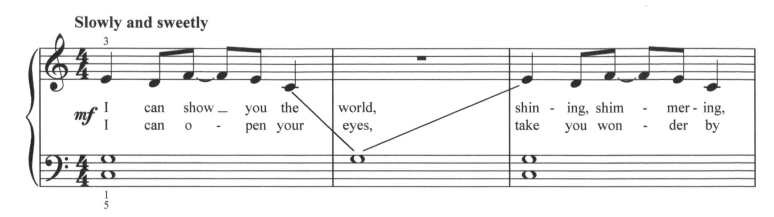

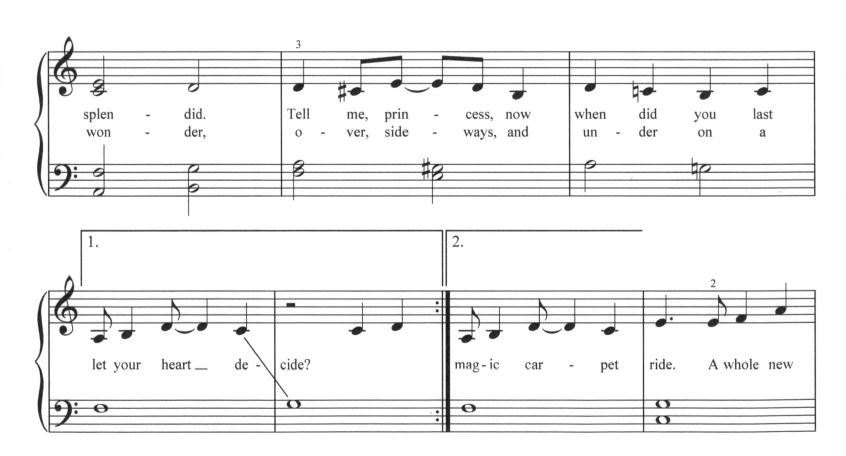

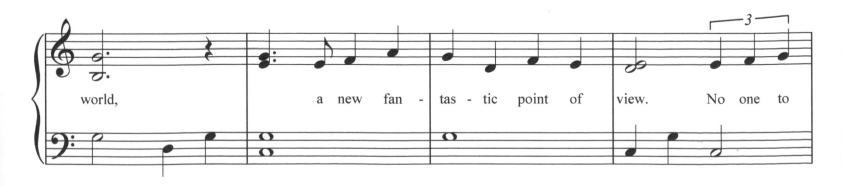

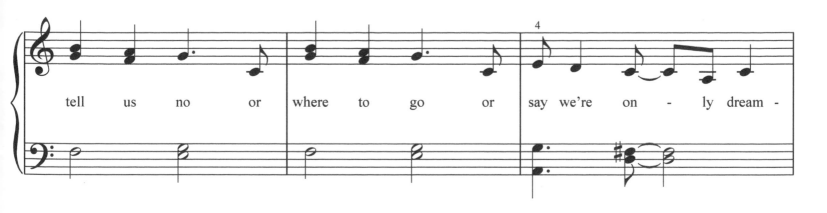

tell us no or where to go or say we're on - ly dream -

ing. A whole new world, a daz - zling place I nev - er

knew. But when I'm way up here it's crys - tal clear that now I'm in a

whole new world with you.

LET IT GO
from FROZEN

Music and Lyrics by KRISTEN ANDERSON-LOPEZ
and ROBERT LOPEZ

Half-time feel

The snow glows white on the moun-tain to-night, _ not a foot-print ___ to be seen. _

A king-dom of i - so - la - tion, and it

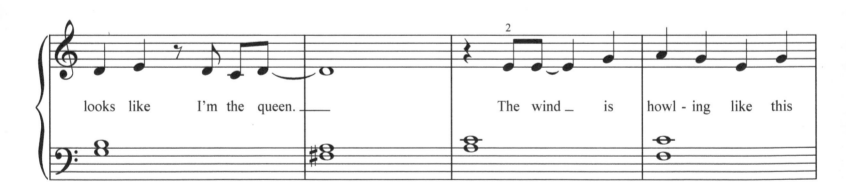

looks like I'm the queen. ___ The wind _ is howl-ing like this

swirl - ing storm in - side. ___ Could-n't keep it in, __

hold it back an - y - more. ___ Let it go, ___ let it go, ___

___ turn a - way ___ and slam _ the __ door. _ I don't _ care _

___ what they're going to __ say, ___ let the storm rage __ on. ___

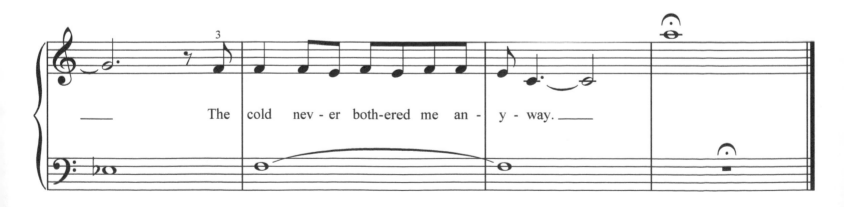

___ The cold nev - er both-ered me an - y - way. ___

YOU'RE WELCOME

from MOANA

Music and Lyrics by
LIN-MANUEL MIRANDA

Moderately fast

I see what's hap-pen-ing, yeah; __

__ you're face to face with great-ness, and it's strange. You don't e-ven know __

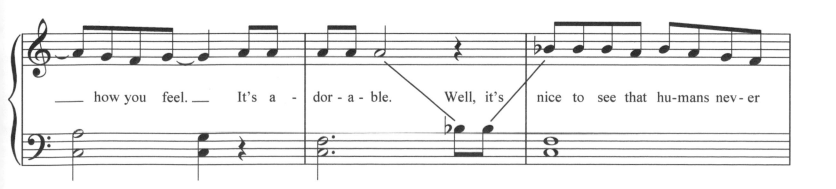

__ how you feel. __ It's a-dor-a-ble. Well, it's nice to see that hu-mans nev-er

change.   O - pen your eyes. ___   Let's __ be - gin. ___   Yes, it's real - ly

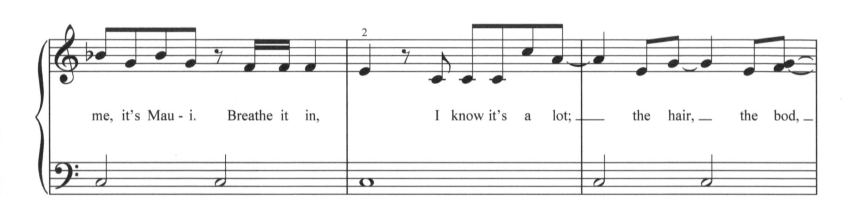

me, it's Mau - i.   Breathe it in,   I know it's a lot; __ the hair, __ the bod, __

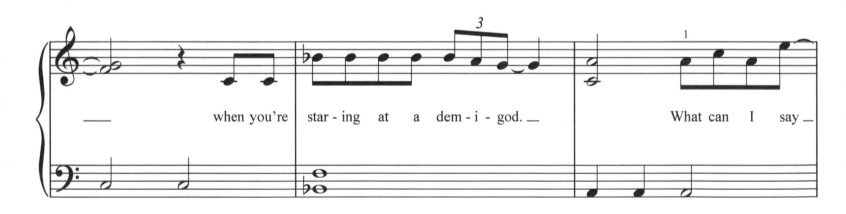

__ when you're star - ing at a dem - i - god. __   What can I say __

__ ex - cept, "You're wel - come,   for the tides, __ the sun, __ the sky?" __

Hey, it's o - kay; ___ it's o - kay: ___ you're wel - come. I'm

just an or - di - nar - y dem - i - guy. ___ Hey, what has two thumbs __

__ and pulled up the sky ___ when you were wad - dl - ing yea high? This guy!

When the nights got cold, ___ who stole __ you fire ___ from down be - low? You're

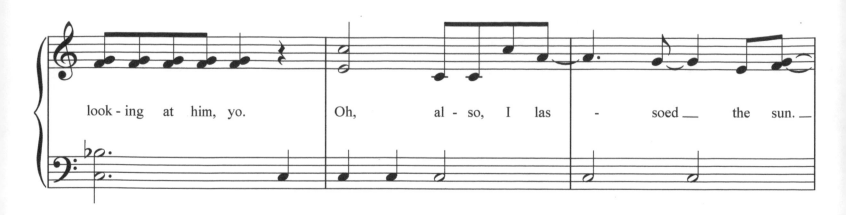

look - ing at him, yo. Oh, al - so, I las - soed the sun.

You're wel - come. To stretch your days and bring you fun.

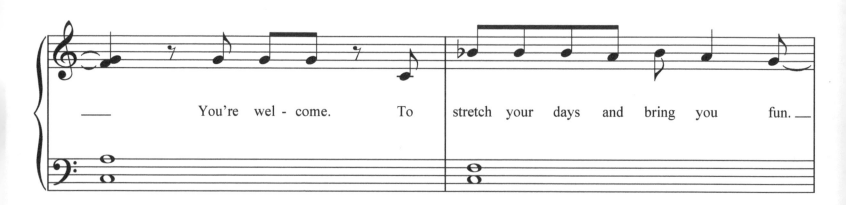

Al - so, I har - nessed the breeze. You're wel - come. To

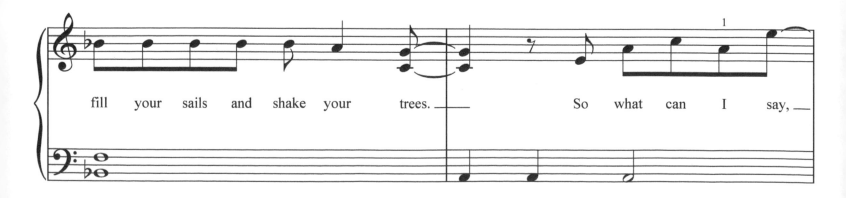

fill your sails and shake your trees. So what can I say,

ex - cept, __ "You're wel - come, for the is - lands I pulled __ from the sea?" __

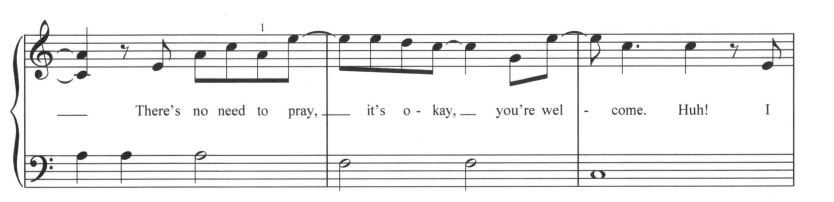

__ There's no need to pray, __ it's o - kay, __ you're wel - come. Huh! I

guess it's just my way of be - ing me! __ You're wel - come! You're wel -

- come! And thank you.

8vb

KISS THE GIRL
from THE LITTLE MERMAID

Music by ALAN MENKEN
Lyrics by HOWARD ASHMAN

Moderately

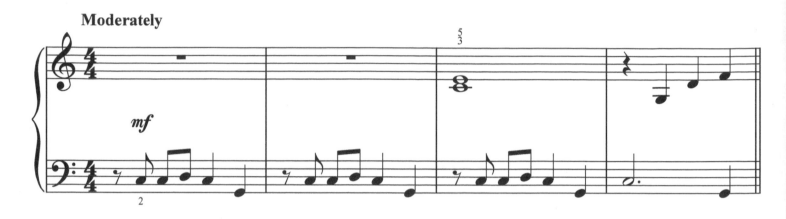

There you see her sit-ting there a-cross the way.

She don't got a lot to say,___ but there's some-thing a-bout her.

And you don't know why,___ but you're dy-ing to try. You wan-na kiss the girl.

Yes, you want her. Look at her, you know you

do. Pos - si - ble she wants you, too.___ There is one way to

ask her. It don't take a word,___ not a sin - gle word,___ go on and

kiss the girl. Sha la la la la,

my oh my,___ look like the boy too shy.___ Ain't gon - na kiss the girl.

Sha la la la la la, ain't that sad.___ Ain't it a shame, too bad.___ He gon - na

miss the girl.___

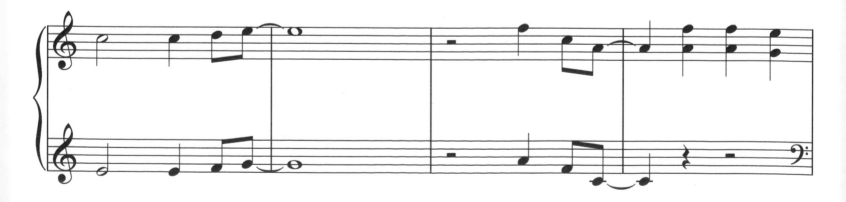

Now's your mo - ment, float - ing in a blue la -

goon. Boy, you bet - ter do it soon, no time will be

bet - ter. She don't say a word ___ and she

won't say a word un - til you kiss the girl.

Sha la la la la la, don't be scared. ___ You got the mood pre - pared, ___ go on and
Sha la la la la la, float a - long. ___ And lis - ten to the song, ___ the song say

kiss the girl. Sha la la la la la, don't stop now. ___ Don't try to
kiss the girl. Sha la la la la the mu - sic play. ___ Do what the

hide it how＿ you wan - na   kiss the girl.   kiss the girl.
mu - sic say.＿ You got - ta

You've got to   kiss the girl.   You wan - na

kiss the girl.   You've got - ta   kiss the girl.

Go on and   kiss the girl.

CAN YOU FEEL THE LOVE TONIGHT

from THE LION KING

Music by ELTON JOHN
Lyrics by TIM RICE

Moderately

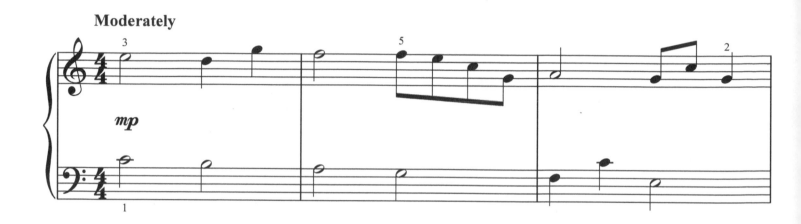

There's a calm sur - ren - der to the rush of day,
There's a time for ev - 'ry - one if they on - ly learn,

when the heat of the rol - ling world can be turned a - way.
that the twist - ing ka - lei - do - scope moves us all in turn.

55

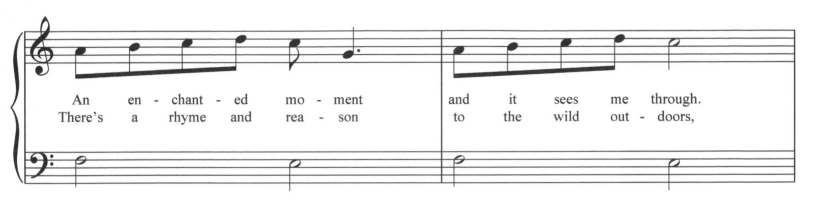

An en - chant - ed mo - ment and it sees me through.
There's a rhyme and rea - son to the wild out - doors,

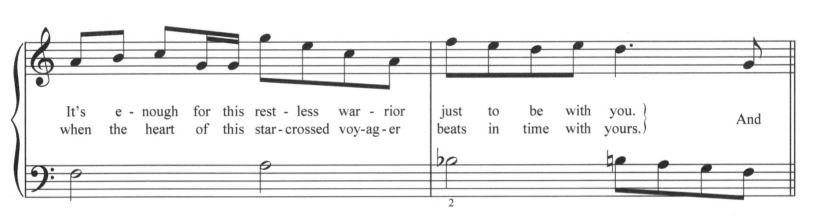

It's e - nough for this rest - less war - rior just to be with you.
when the heart of this star - crossed voy - ag - er beats in time with yours.
And

can you feel the love to - night? _ It is where we
can you feel the love to - night, _ how it's laid to

are.
rest? It's e - nough for this wide - eyed wan - der - er
It's e - nough to make kings and va - ga - bonds be -

COLORS OF THE WIND
from POCAHONTAS

Music by ALAN MENKEN
Lyrics by STEPHEN SCHWARTZ

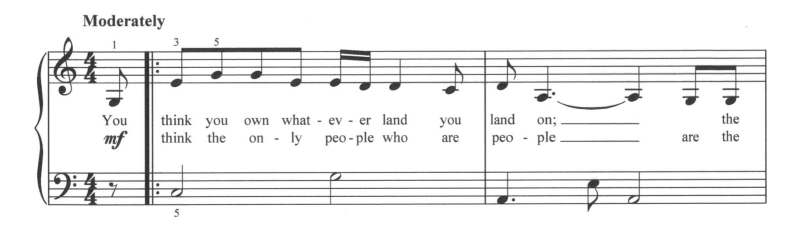

58

things ____ you nev - er knew ____ you nev - er knew. Have you

ev - er heard the wolf cry to the blue corn moon or { asked the grin-ning bob - cat why he / let the ea - gle tell you where he's

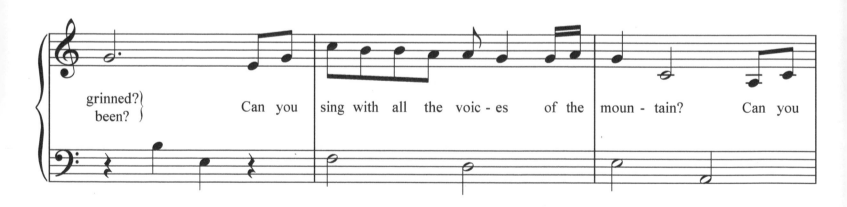

grinned? } / been? } Can you sing with all the voic - es of the moun - tain? Can you

To Coda

paint with all the col - ors of the wind? Can you paint with all the col-ors of the

wind? _____ Come run the hid - den pine trails of the
rain - storm and the riv - er are my

for - est, _____ come taste the sun-sweet ber - ries of the earth, come
broth - ers: _____ the her - on and the ot - ter are my friends; and

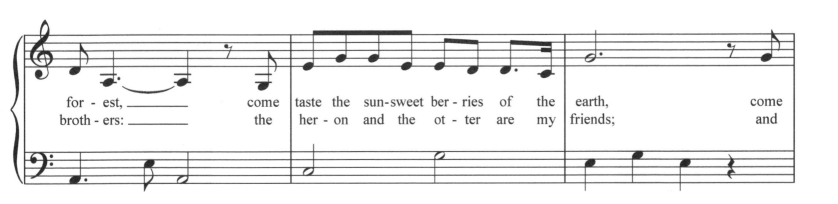

1.

roll in all the rich - es all a - round you, _____ and for once nev - er won - der what they're
we are all con - nect - ed to each oth - er _____ in a

2.

D.S. al Coda

worth. The cir - cle, in a hoop that nev - er ends. Have you

CODA

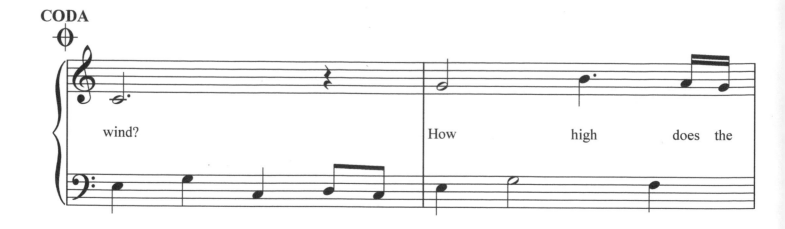

wind?　　　How　high　does　the

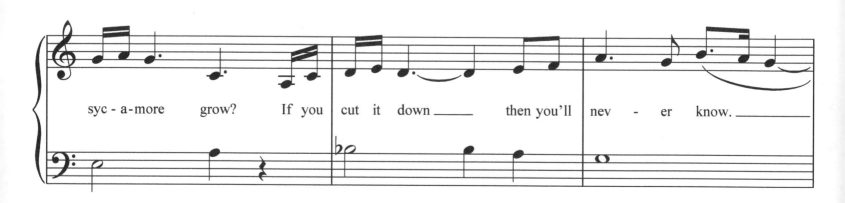

syc - a-more　grow?　If　you　cut　it　down＿＿　then　you'll　nev - er　know.＿＿

＿　　And　you'll　nev - er　hear　the wolf　cry　to　the　blue　corn　moon,　for

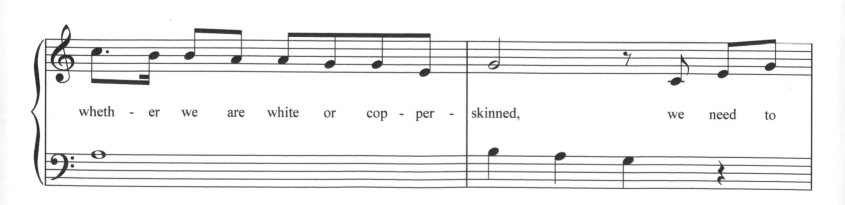

wheth - er　we　are　white　or　cop - per - skinned,　　　we　need　to

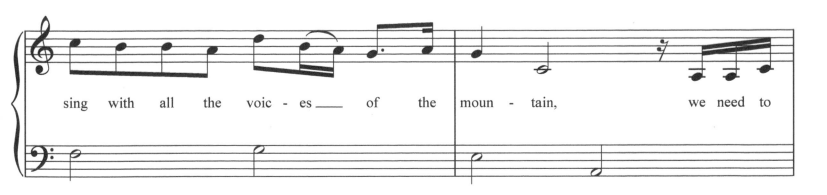

sing with all the voic - es ____ of the moun - tain, we need to

paint with all the col-ors of the wind. You can own the earth _ and still all you'll

own is earth un - til, you can paint with all the col - ors of the

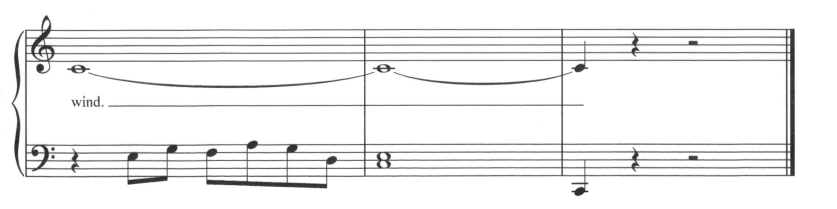

wind. ____

WRITTEN IN THE STARS

from AIDA

Music by ELTON JOHN
Lyrics by TIM RICE

Slowly

Here I am to tell __ you we can nev - er meet a - gain.

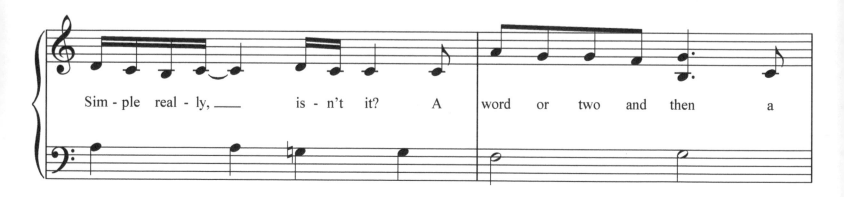

Sim - ple real - ly, __ is - n't it? A word or two and then a

life-time of not know-ing where or how or why or when. You think of me or speak of me or

won-der what be - fell ___ the some-one you once loved ___ so long a - go ___ so well. _

Nev - er won - der what ___ I'll feel as liv - ing shuf - fles by.
Noth - ing can be al - tered. Oh, there is noth - ing to de - cide.

You don't have to ask ___ me and I need not re - ply.
No es - cape, no change of heart, nor an - y - place to hide.

Ev - 'ry mo - ment of ___ my life from now un - til I die
You are all I'll ev - er want but this I am de - nied.

I will think or dream of you and fail ____ to un-der-stand ____ how a
Some-times in my dark-est thoughts I wish ____ I nev-er learned ____ what it

per - fect love can be ____ con - found - ed out of hand. Is it
is to be in love ____ and have that love re - turned.

writ - ten in the stars? ____ Are we pay - ing for some crime? ____ Is that

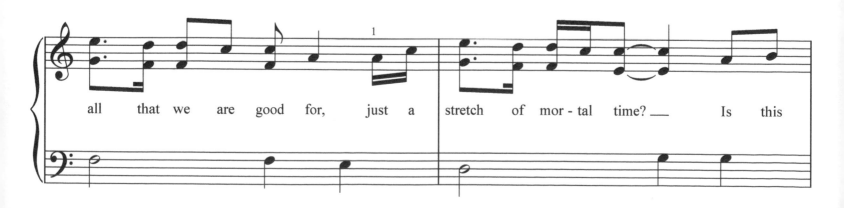

all that we are good for, just a stretch of mor - tal time? ____ Is this

God's ex - per - i - ment ____ in which we have no say? ____ In

which we're giv - en par - a - dise, but on - ly for a day. ____

on - ly for a day. ____

rit.

YO HO

(A Pirate's Life for Me)

from Disney Parks' Pirates of the Caribbean attraction

Words by XAVIER ATENCIO
Music by GEORGE BRUNS

In a robust manner

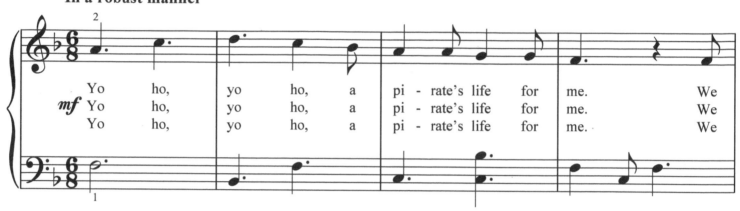

3. up me 'eart-ies, yo ho. We're ras-cals and scoun-drels, we're / beg-gars and blight-ers and

vil-lains and knaves. Drink up me 'eart-ies, yo ho. We're dev-ils and black sheep, we're / ne'er-do-well cads. Drink up me 'eart-ies, yo ho. Aye, but __ we're loved by our

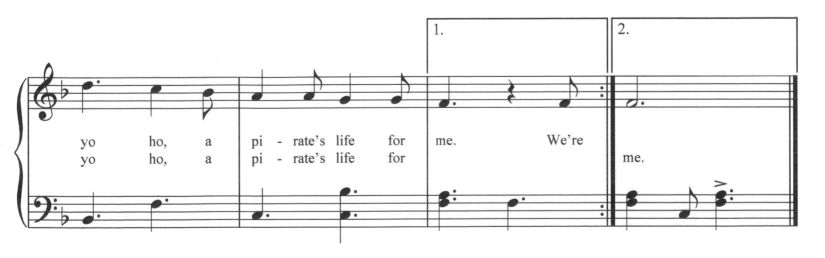

real-ly bad eggs. Drink up me 'eart-ies, yo ho. Yo ho, / mom-mies 'n' dads. Drink up me 'eart-ies, yo ho. Yo ho,

yo ho, a pi-rate's life for me. We're / yo ho, a pi-rate's life for me.

1. **2.**

THE WORLD ES MI FAMILIA

from COCO

Music by GERMAINE FRANCO
Lyrics by ADRIAN MOLINA

Moderately fast, in 2

ñor - es. To be here with you to - night _____ brings me

joy! Que al - e - grí - a! ____ For this mu - sic is my

lan - guage and the world es ____ mi fa - mi - lia. ____

For this mu - sic is my

BIBBIDI-BOBBIDI-BOO
(The Magic Song)
from CINDERELLA

Words by JERRY LIVINGSTON
Music by MACK DAVID and AL HOFFMAN

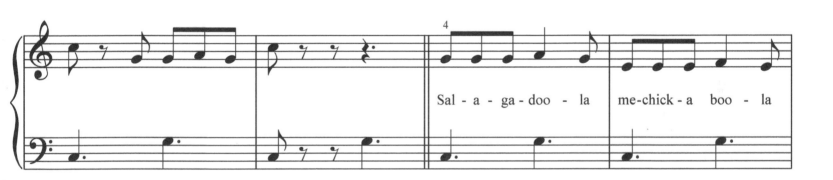

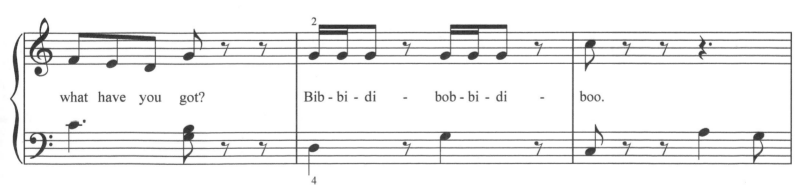

Sal - a - ga - doo - la   me - chick - a boo - la   bib - bi - di - bob - bi - di -

boo.   It - 'll do mag - ic, be - lieve it or not!

rit.

Bib - bi - di - bob - bi - di - boo.   Now, sal - a - ga - doo - la

a tempo

means   me - chick - a - boo - la - roo,   but the thing - a - ma - bob that

does the job is bib - bi - di - bob - bi - di - boo. Boo!

Sal - a - ga - doo - la me - chick - a boo - la bib - bi - di - bob - bi - di -

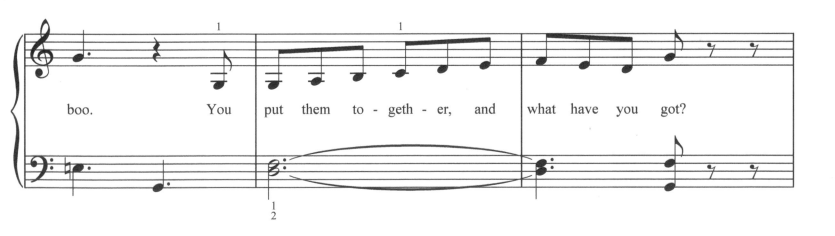

boo. You put them to - geth - er, and what have you got?

Bib - bi - di - bob - bi - di - boo. Sal - a - ga - doo - la

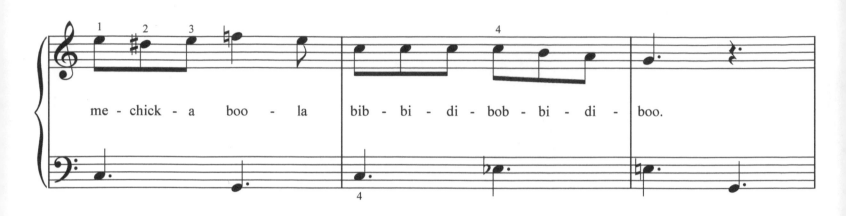

me - chick - a boo - la bib - bi - di - bob - bi - di - boo.

Put 'em to - geth - er, and what have you got? Bib - bi - di - bob - bi - di -

boo. Now, sal - a - ga - doo - la means me - chick - a - boo - la -

roo, but the thing - a - ma - bob that does the job is

bib - bi - di - bob - bi - di - boo! Sal - a - ga - doo - la

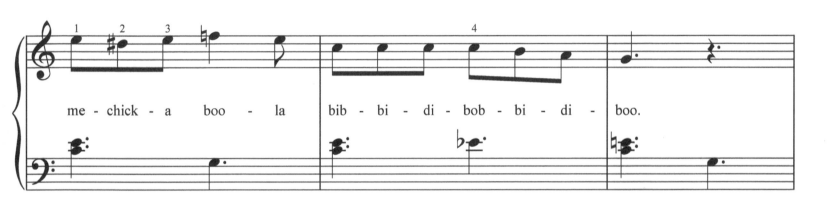

me - chick - a boo - la bib - bi - di - bob - bi - di - boo.

Put 'em to - geth - er, and what have you got? Bib - bi - di - bob - bi - di...

Bib - bi - di - bob - bi - di... Bib - bi - di - bob - bi - di - boo! _____

CRUELLA DE VIL
from 101 DALMATIANS

Words and Music by
MEL LEVEN

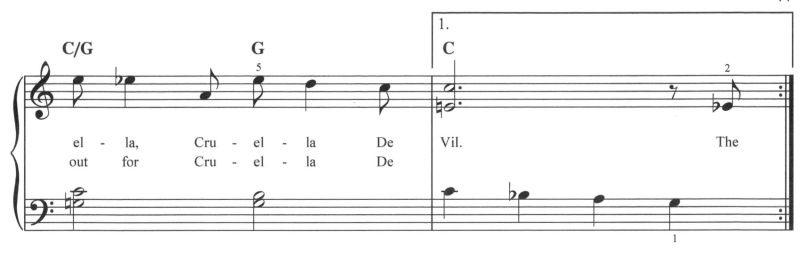

el - la, Cru - el - la De Vil. The
out for Cru - el - la De

Vil. At first, you think Cru - el - la is a dev - il, but

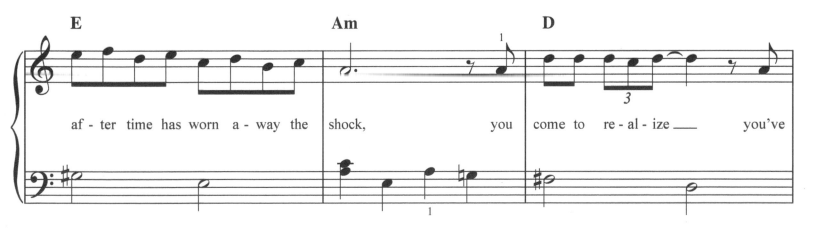

af - ter time has worn a - way the shock, you come to re - al - ize __ you've

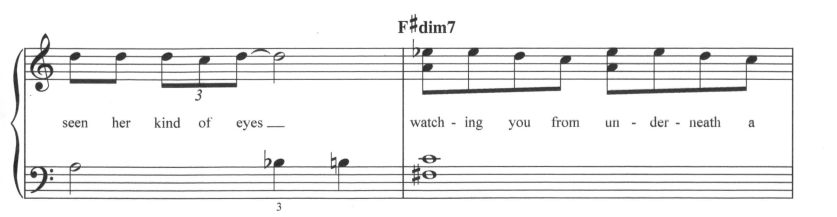

seen her kind of eyes __ watch - ing you from un - der - neath a

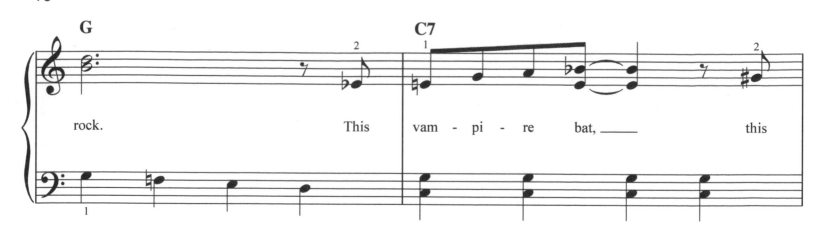

rock.   This vam - pi - re bat, _____ this

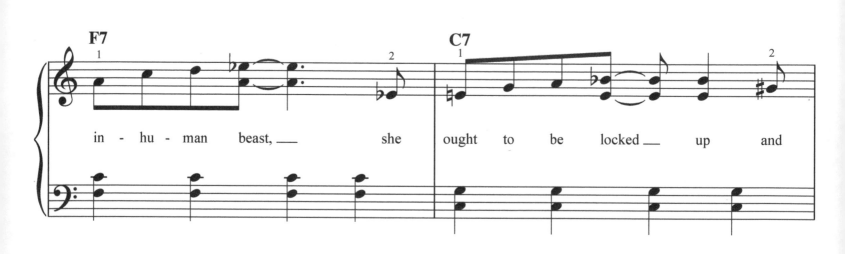

in - hu - man beast, __ she ought to be locked __ up and

nev - er re - leased. __ The world was such a whole - some place un -

til   Cru - el - la, Cru - el - la De Vil.

FRIEND LIKE ME

from ALADDIN

Music by ALAN MENKEN
Lyrics by HOWARD ASHMAN

Moderately

Well, A - li

Ba - ba had them for - ty thieves. Sche - her - a - za - de had a thou - sand

tales. But, mas - ter, you're in luck 'cause up your sleeves you got a

brand of mag - ic nev - er fails. You got some pow - er in your

cor - ner now, __ some heav - y am - mu - ni - tion in your camp. You got some

punch, pi - zazz, ya - hoo and how. __ See, all you got - ta do is rub that

lamp. And I'll __ say Mis - ter A - lad - din sir, __ what will your pleas - ure

be? Let me take your or - der, jot it down. You ain't

nev - er had a friend like me. No no no. Life is your

res - tau - rant ___ and I'm your mai - tre d.' C' - mon

whis - per what it is you want. You ain't nev - er had a friend like

me. Yes, sir, we pride our - selves on ser - vice. You're the

boss, the king, the shah. Say what you wish. ___ It's

yours! True dish! ___ How 'bout a lit - tle more bak - la - va? _____

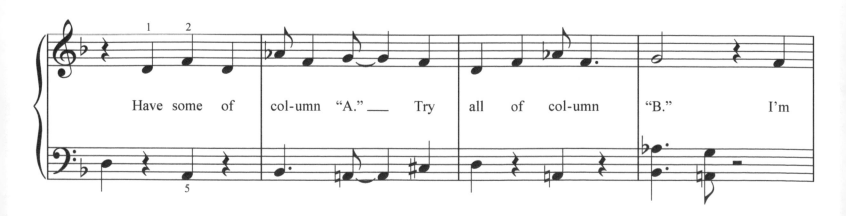

Have some of col-umn "A." ___ Try all of col-umn "B." I'm

in the mood to help you, dude, you ain't nev - er had a friend like

me. Wa - ah - ah. Oh my.

Wa - ah - ah. No no. Wa - ah - ah.

Na na na.

YOU'VE GOT A FRIEND IN ME
from TOY STORY

Music and Lyrics by
RANDY NEWMAN

You've got a friend in me.
You've got a friend in me.

You've got a friend in me.
You've got a friend in me.

When the road looks
You got trou - bles, then

rough a - head _____ and you're   miles _____ and miles _____ from your
I got 'em too. _____   There is - n't an - y - thing

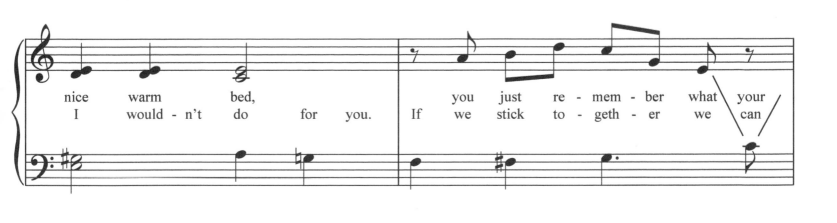

Now some oth - er folks might be a lit - tle bit smart - er than I am,

big - ger and strong - er too. May - be. But none of them will

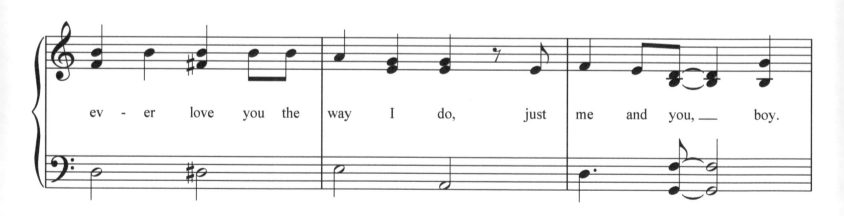

ev - er love you the way I do, just me and you, — boy.

And as the years go by, our friend-ship will nev - er

die.　You're gon - na see　it's our　des - ti - ny.

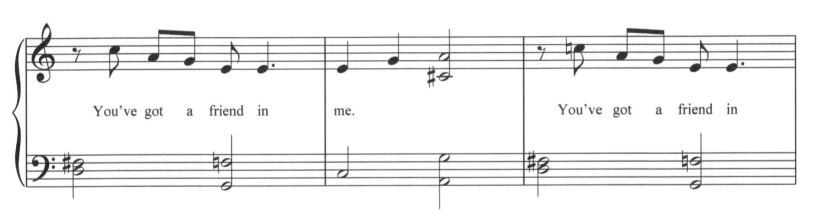

You've got　a friend in　me.　You've got　a friend in

me.　You've got　a friend　in　me.

rit.

SEQUENTIAL

PIANO SONGBOOK SERIES

Pianists of all levels can enjoy current and classic hits with Sequential Piano Songs! Starting with the easiest arrangements (hands alone, very simple rhythms) and progressing in order of difficulty (hands together, syncopated rhythms and moving around the keyboard), these supplemental songbooks are a terrific resource for improving music reading and piano skills from the very first page.

SEQUENTIAL CHRISTMAS PIANO SONGS

26 Holiday Favorites Carefully Selected and Arranged in Order of Difficulty

All I Want for Christmas Is My Two Front Teeth • Believe • The Christmas Song (Chestnuts Roasting on an Open Fire) • Frosty the Snow Man • It's Beginning to Look like Christmas • Jingle Bell Rock • Mary, Did You Know? • Rudolph the Red-Nosed Reindeer • White Christmas • and more.

00294929 Easy Piano..$16.99

SEQUENTIAL DISNEY PIANO SONGS

24 Easy Favorites Carefully Selected and Arranged in Order of Difficulty

Be Our Guest • Can You Feel the Love Tonight • Chim Chim Cher-ee • A Dream Is a Wish Your Heart Makes • Evermore • I See the Light • Kiss the Girl • Let It Go • A Whole New World (Aladdin's Theme) • The World Es Mi Familia • You've Got a Friend in Me • and more.

00294870 Easy Piano..$16.99

SEQUENTIAL JAZZ PIANO SONGS

26 Easy Favorites Carefully Selected and Arranged in Order of Difficulty

All the Things You Are • Autumn Leaves • Bye Bye Blackbird • Fly Me to the Moon (In Other Words) • I Got Rhythm • It Could Happen to You • Misty • My Funny Valentine • Satin Doll • Stardust • Take Five • The Way You Look Tonight • When I Fall in Love • and more.

00286967 Easy Piano..$16.99

SEQUENTIAL KIDS' PIANO SONGS

24 Easy Favorites Carefully Selected and Arranged in Order of Difficulty

Best Day of My Life • Can You Feel the Love Tonight • The Chicken Dance • Do-Re-Mi • Happy Birthday to You • If You're Happy and You Know It • Let It Go • Sing • Star Wars (Main Theme) • Take Me Out to the Ball Game • This Land Is Your Land • Tomorrow • A Whole New World • and more.

00286602 Easy Piano..$16.99

SEQUENTIAL POP PIANO SONGS

24 Easy Favorites Carefully Selected and Arranged in Order of Difficulty

All My Loving • Beauty and the Beast • Brave • Daydream Believer • Feel It Still • Hallelujah • Love Me Tender • One Call Away • Over the Rainbow • Perfect • Rolling in the Deep • Shake It Off • Stay with Me • Thinking Out Loud • Unchained Melody • and more.

00279889 Easy Piano..$16.99

Disney Characters and Artwork TM & © 2019 Disney
Prices, contents, and availability subject to change without notice.

HAL•LEONARD®
www.halleonard.com